# A Pineapple and an Old Yellow Curtain

A collection of poems by Laraine Kentridge Lasdon

# A Pineapple and an Old Yellow Curtain

copyright
© 2023

ISBN 979-8-218-34041-4

# Table of Contents

The Good Moon                                      1

The Ghosts of Lime Kiln Road                       2

The Age of Humans                                  3

Wing of a Hawk                                     4

Garden of Blue Pills                               5

Confections                                        6

In The Company of Birds                            7

Musings on Mango, Tea, and an Orange Flame         8

Hey! Hey!                                          9

Yellow Curtain                                     10

Last Kiss                                          11

Thunder Bay                                        12

Diagnosis                                          13

Cloud-Kinship                                      14

*Huge thanks to my husband and daughter
for their unwavering support!*

# *The Good Moon*

I wallow in the luscious marrow
of self-pity. It's comfortable
hiding in the past. I can cry here.
A sliver of moonbeam
gleams on bleak tears.

Time, the linchpin of youth, has come loose,
like the moon drifting away from earth.
Childhood traumas, loveless hurts,
futile in the face of a finite future.

Float in the night sky, dear friend.
Travel there, to the good moon,
before time unravels, soon to end.

Moonlight curls around fingers and hair.
Time is impartial in this rarefied air.
The old man's rays are paler than gold.
Seen up close. Quite frail and old.
Are we not all a bit like this?
I stroke his dear face, bestow a kiss,
just as the sun rises to take his place.

## The Ghosts of Lime Kiln Road

Summon your demons, devils, and wraiths,
visit moments of hurt and loss.
Replay what might have been, wrestle with regrets,
Do "if only" scenes haunt your past?

I follow the faint ribbon of sand on Mackinac Island,
lined with sugar maple tree, aspen and lilac.
Wild lily of the valley, its fragrant musk, from dusk to dawn,
clings to lichen and headstone,
in the old cemetery at the end of Lime Kiln Road.

I am as ghostly as the local specters.
The fine young military boy,
eyes wild and strange,
wandering across the old rifle range,
striving to collect his remit.
Payment for the murder he did not commit.

Or darling Miss Biddle, only eight years old.
They handed her Mama her green Christmas coat.
Drowned when the ice cracked, no-one saw.
Lost in a snowstorm on the island of Mackinac.

Ghosts are so practical. They wander, they howl,
always in the same place, always the same sound.
Patient in time eternal, that their fate will dissolve or resolve.

My earthly body moves through life,
restless in my quest to change the past.
Spirits moan, I am not lost.
I close my eyes and dance with my ghosts.

## The Age of Humans

Waterways, red cliffs,
ancient underwater caves,
back to the Pangea age,
continents fused as one.
I stand in the stardust
of a million-year-old memory,
a flutter of songbirds,
a bouquet of warblers,
the wild swoop of blue jays.
Hummingbirds check me out.
My breath hovers over crimson wildflowers.

Long before the idea of a kiss,
when love was mystery,
the earth entered its quaternary period,
the age of humans.
A time of gestation, anticipation,
the Great Lakes birthing,
hawks soaring, the first migration.
All we see of that coded mapping
are faint skeletal imprints,
visible in glacial rock formations.

The stone I cradle, a mountain remnant,
honors the ancestral presence
my encounter with raw existence.

The lake shivers as falcons dive,
beaks and talons fisted and footed.
A drop of water touches my face.
Profound. As much as a human caress.

# Wing of a Hawk

The signal
to leave is called out urgently.
Blue jays spin, whistle, and gurgle.
Heralds of the gray days of winter.

We climb Hawk Ridge Observatory hill.
The rough benches, wooden table, a simple tabernacle.
It's a late summer day,
tinged with the soft reds of Fall.
The lake swells, delicate white froth
hushes and bubbles caressing the shore.

Our guide lifts something curious
out of a dusty old box.
In her arms is a single great wing.
With gentle gesture she invites us in.
Birdsong relaying migration routes
form a choir as we silently approach.

This was a killing wing.
Ruthless in its resolute trajectory of the dive,
grasp of bloodied vole to nourish
his brood, squawking from their cliff-edge nest.
Each feather feels strong, indestructible,
yet, this hawk was found with wings outstretched,
a span of six feet end-to-end,
neck broken on the golden sand.

I stroke the black and grey feathers.
Thin-ribbed architecture smooth, cool,
the skeletal structure rustling, lifting,
lifting as if it might suddenly take off.

The corpse-wing caught the next gust of wind
carrying the hawk-spirit on thermal spirals.
High in the pale of blue sky a hawk wheels and cries,
casting a shadow onto the very spot her mate died.

Mourned by his love. Majestic in death.
I learned about life, that day at Hawk Ridge.

# Garden of Blue Pills

Curled up on the floor.
In the middle of the day.
I dream this story:

"I visit my garden each morning
clawing at the ground to see
if the unused pills I found
in my mother's pill boxes,
and planted, had produced
a rose or purple Phlox.
I buried her tablet boxes,
buried them, buried anger,
buried frustration, buried fury
in these improvised coffins.
I lined the miniature graves
with crushed blue velvet,
(the lining of her case of tiny forks
used at four o'clock tea-time).

Treading through wet grass,
rootling through fertile soil,
I saw, without surprise,
blue pills growing wild,
scattered and whimsical,
my mother decorating
the strange garden
with silver cake forks
tied with ribbons."

I make a cup of tea,
cut a slice of cake,
and eat it with a small,
English fork nestled
in a blue velvet-lined box.

# *Confections*

Everything I am seems to be someone else

Imagine a memory mirror
framed with pearlescent medallions.

The mirror reflects a young girl,
always alone, insubstantial,
dressed in spun cotton candy,

sweet, hoping to be liked
in her fairy floss robe.

The mirror cracks.
she pulls the sharp shards

from the shattered glass
with her bare hands.

Crystals splinter, crack
onto the stone floor.

Her hands are bloody.
Is she crying. The young girl.

Everything I am belongs to me.
Everything I seem to be, I am.
There is no mirror.

## In The Company of Birds

My eyes are red,
red, like the red-red wingtips
of my two morning birds.
The simian stain
of my human graceless,
sorrow and pain
seeps into the noble architecture
of their nest, but no blemish
can dim its rosy stems.

Morning follows morning,
seductive mist full chill.
I sit on a cold stone wall
under flustered, verdant ferns,
a fugitive sly thing,
thin breath panting,
through wet loose lips,
watching the red birds
fly from oak to cable
without guile, willing
their tangled grace
to nest in me.

I feel the tremor
of wing and heart.
A choir of birdsong
stirs the moist fog of dawn,
in delicate harmony
with my cowardly voice.

Morning after morning
in the company of birds
uncorrupted by futility,
I learn at last, to claim audacity.

Oh! So this is it! I can fly!

And I laughed so hard,
I cried.

# *Musings on Mango, Tea,*
# *and an Orange Flame*

### Mango Memories

I take a ripe mango,
mash the insides with plump thumb,
but not so much that I break the skin,
the flesh inside is broken down
I suck out the pulp
tropical, on a bright orange morning

### Teaspoon of Dry Tea Leaves in a Cup

Boiling water drizzles
perfumed orange brew
tea leaves curl,
cradled in the bottom
of the cup
they whisper the future
of fullness
at 4 o'clock

### The Orange Flame

I have no memory of lighting candles
of welcoming the sabbath bride
of murmuring a prayer about
the sweetness of the grape of the vine
I strike the match
the orange flame wavers and flares
in this moment the sun sets.

## Hey! Hey!

Hey! Hey! Open those doors.
Or let *me* heave against wood, iron, etched glass.
I *embrace* the cracked shatter,
the warped lintel that bends,
and falls on my piney shoulders
like an old Saxon shawl. The twisted keyhole winks
with a pale pool of light in the lock.

Hey! Hey! I feel skin tear, splinters
drill into blood cavern, thrill
to a flash of pain where nothing matters.
Puckered lips, air whistling
through broken teeth, gutted
graveyard, a life almost extinct,
until with final grunt,
the door opens

into a passion of tall trees.
Moist green moss
seen through shards of glass,
wraps around my arms
and heals my thirsty soul.

## *Yellow Curtain*

flowing undulating
calligraphy of the sea
announcing sunset
inviting in the evening moon
cone of light on a sea salted street
brilliant as the theme park at the beach
ramshackle shouting
doors slam shut
percussive punctuation
ends the essay of the day

I close the old yellow curtain
stumble-mumble tired
half lidded eyes
un-kissed lips dry
I suck on the remains
of a pineapple, finger-flick
blueberries that scatter
like glass marbles
in a pinball machine
sticking to the splinters
of the carved wooden table

sun-blaze hot sculpts
the humble lining
of the curtain
pulled open
to greet another morning
a sand-carved
seagull feather
ripples time
with a light touch
it might be your spirit
moving through
we never had much
which is fine as things go
but now I don't even have you.

# Last Kiss

My love and I
wrote our biographies in the
exuberance of a breeze,
in the scent
of moss and sand.
Flying leaves, dying leaves,
stirred up sticks,
nests
clinging to bare branches.
Elements as architecture.

We watched birds,
trailed fingers in ponds,
feeling joy
in the humor
and playfulness of the leaves.

Our naked feet flirted with the grass.
We licked lips, felt wicked,
flicked our hair in the wind. Tasted the grit of Fall.

Those were wonderful days
when we kissed, as if we were
the very first lovers
to sigh and murmur.

We could have chosen romance.
Autumn as a beginning not an end.
We walked to the Gare du St. Marie
aware of the hiss of the train.

Extraordinary.
How sweet the poison
of his last kiss.

## *Thunder Bay*

His old cap was on backwards
like the kids hanging out at the pier,
sunglasses winked blue
"Are you from here" he asked,
companionably.  Weathered face,
dialect like he swallowed six seagulls.
"No" I said. "I knew it" he said,
and another gull nested in his gullet.
Roses, bees and circles of rock formed the Spirit Garden.
Behind us Lake Superior stretched into the distance,
sky-winds tossing moods out to the lighthouse.
We stood there, the old man and I.

# Diagnosis

I turn to mankind's endeavors, intuition,
to gain insight into my afflictions.
Bibles, books, blogs, Dante's Hell,
babbling towers, bridal gowns
of plaster and bronze,
none seemed to wield the magic wand.

It was only recently I was diagnosed with "Life".
I realized how little the health gods
understood what a patient goes through.
With all knowledge of skin, bones, and nails,
the profundity of the human experience
is where I find the malaise,

The prescription was there,
an unopened vessel.
Wrestling, falling,
collapsing imaginary walls,
smoothing rumpled dreams,
the stale cork crumbled.
I allowed healing in.

I understood what I could become
with the tenured remains
of the swiftly draining sands.
I knew the cure: re-birth, accept.
"Heal thyself." The age-old concept.

A home, friends, the bleak past,
I saw it all!
There was the red cardinal
in the tangle of bare trees,
in plain sight now that I see.
Just there, everywhere,
it was all you, it was all me.
It was all the meanings of Hineini:
I am here. I **am** here. I am **here**.

# Cloud-Kinship

I feel a kinship with the clouds.
I cherish my relationship
with their backlit iridescence,
their churning journeys
swirling towards worlds
that I will never know.

The kinfolk of my life

I think, were never fluid
or forgiving or shapeshifting.
The memory I have
is of black-eyes,
wardens of a locked box
of dreams

not at all like a cloud,
white, silver, melting rose.
I wished for a dawn of velvet,
a downy robe of snow-cloud,
a horizon of my own,
a key of gold
to open the drab box,
dun color, rusted lock.

sweet cloud,
essence of freedom.
We are cousins are we not?
Older now I feel more like you.
An incandescent flicker,
a final wisp of mist.

www.ingramcontent.com/pod-product-compliance
Lightning Source LLC
Chambersburg PA
CBHW051254120626
46547CB00014B/1939